Duecentomila

Duecentomila

kai fig taddei

Playwrights Canada Press

TORONTO

LIBRARY AND ARCHIVES CANADA CATALOGUING IN PUBLICATION
Title: Duecentomila / Kai Fig Taddei.
Names: Taddei, Kai Fig, author.
Description: A play.
Identifiers: Canadiana (print) 20220397198 | Canadiana (ebook) 20220397252
 | ISBN 9780369103826 (softcover) | ISBN 9780369103840 (PDF)
 | ISBN 9780369103833 (HTML)
Classification: LCC PS8639.A245 D84 2022 | DDC C812/.6—DC23

Playwrights Canada Press operates on land which is the ancestral home of the Anishinaabe Nations (Ojibwe / Chippewa, Odawa, Potawatomi, Algonquin, Sault-eaux, Nipissing, and Mississauga), the Wendat, and the members of the Haudenosaunee Confederacy (Mohawk, Oneida, Onondaga, Cayuga, Seneca, and Tuscarora), as well as Metis and Inuit peoples. It always was and always will be Indigenous land.

We acknowledge the support of the Canada Council for the Arts, the Ontario Arts Council (OAC), Ontario Creates, and the Government of Canada for our publishing activities.

 Canada Council for the Arts Conseil des arts du Canada ONTARIO ARTS COUNCIL CONSEIL DES ARTS DE L'ONTARIO an Ontario government agency un organisme du gouvernement de l'Ontario

 Canadä ONTARIO CREATES | ONTARIO CRÉATIF

for Alexa, Julie & Emily—better late than never!

for my mom: you taught me to be grateful for my chosen family. you also taught me not to take bullshit from my biological one. love you.

and for Paolo: we didn't have enough time together. but I'm told I inherited your intensity, your stubbornness, your passion. scorpio solidarity.

Foreword

By Paula Wing

How do you grow a new life inside yourself, alone?

This huge question is at the heart of this buoyant and beautiful play. The characters are living the fraught, perilous moment between childhood and adulthood. As the playwright puts it:

There's too much happening at once. Inside. Outside.

Each of these characters wants to determine their own identities in their own time, in their own way, by the light of their own compass. The play expertly—and hilariously—reveals how even well-meaning friends must allow each other the breadth and the breath to make their own choices.

And speaking of hilarious, what is remarkable about kai fig taddei's writing is the delicious humour they find in these intense struggles. *Duecentomila* is a heart-centred comedy about self, about the selves we take on and discard, as well as the selves we step into and come to fully own.

My own first encounter with the play was serendipitous. After Artistic Director Nina Lee Aquino brought me on as a replacement dramaturge during a development process at Factory Theatre, kai and I met on a kind of dramaturgical blind date in a café. I was immediately engaged by their intellectual energy, easy humour, and passionate commitment to storytelling. The chemistry held. The process went swimmingly.

A year later, kai asked me to direct a staged reading of the play at Ergo Pink Fest in Toronto, a showcase for writers of marginalized genders. The depth of the comedy was revealed to me in rehearsals for that reading. It's funny on the page, but you don't get all the layers of humour until you hear it, until actors embody the words. The rehearsal room rang with our laughter and truths emerged, both from the play and from the performers' personal experiences. Their stories—and the rousing audience reaction to the reading—affirmed the need, the hunger for a story like this, so multi-faceted and so honest about what it takes for some of us to come into our own.

I realized that, before working on this play, I had no idea of the range and specificities of trans peoples' experiences. Even in that small group of folks at rehearsal, each person had unique experiences to share, and each path required creativity, bravery, determination, a sense of humour, and an unshakable drive to be one's fullest self. I saw the complex and thrilling task before the characters in a clearer light. As Kat says in the play, they are all trying to:

Make new traditions out of old ones.

To create something new, Kat and Hanna, Eli and Matteo have to really listen to each other, and that, often, involves translation. The play's translations go between one language and another, one culture and another, one identity and another. The act of becoming yourself requires translation too. Everyone here wrestles with the values instilled in them by family and society. What do they hold on to, what do they jettison? What can be rationally explained to other people and what can only be felt and lived? In translation, sometimes even when you find the literally correct definition, you can still be missing the deeper nuances.

I could write two hundred thousand more words about *Duecentomila*, and there are at least two hundred thousand reasons to read it. Let's just say: welcome to the funny, soulful, original work of kai fig taddei. They not only dream of a better world, but their words are also helping to build it.

I will soon be reborn as the most beautiful work of art in the world.

Paula Wing is a playwright, translator, and teacher. Plays in progress include Vox Lumina, *a story centred around medieval mystic Hildegard of Bingen, and* The Cabin, *a play about land and history in cottage country. Paula's adaptation of Josh Funk's picture book* How to Code a Sandcastle *premiered at Thousand Islands Playhouse in 2021. Her most recent translation is* Home *by Mireille Tawfik for Montreal's Imago Theatre. Paula teaches youth in partnership with many organizations including the Gryphon Trio's Listen Up program, Kick Start Arts, Young People's Theatre, and Soulpepper Theatre. She's a sessional professor at the University of Windsor, and the creative writing instructor at the Native Men's Residence in Toronto. Paula is also a sought-after dramaturge, currently working with, among others, Sarena Parmar on* Hunger, *at Tarragon Theatre, and on* Pawâgan *(a Cree adaptation of Shakespeare's* Macbeth*) by Reneltta Arluk for the Stratford Festival.*

Playwright's Notes

It's a hot blue day on unceded ləkʷəŋən and W̱SÁNEĆ territories as I try to write the preface to this play—less than eighteen hours before it's due to the publisher.

The pads of my fingers are sweating and I'm not wearing pants. I moved into a new house a week ago and my office is barely unpacked. Bubble wrap and dirty clothes and broken glass all over the floor. A little blue quilt embroidered by a human I briefly loved sits on my desk and tells me to KEEP GOING, but all I can think is, *Fuck. How am I ever going to hit send?* All these unfinished thoughts. All these rewrites I've never workshopped. I feel like I have a big red flashing IMPOSTER sign on my forehead.

One of my partners loves to tease me for being a perfectionist, and there's something to that—something to do with capitalist modes of production and whiteness and class (*And maybe*, a dear friend gently points out, *trauma and mental health and fear? . . .*)—but it's *also* to do with the immutability of print. Immutability: it makes me uncomfortable. Soul-prickling, nausea-inducing *deep* discomfort. For obvious as well as private reasons. Especially when it comes to a play like this—a play that's invested in exploring the mutability of gender and spirituality and family and self and and and . . .

My neighbours are watering their gardenias as I sit here, heart hammering, thinking about sharing this thing that's not biographical but not *not* biographical.

This unruly, unfinished *me* thing.

Okay. Let's make these anxieties concrete. "Show, don't tell" and all that shit.

An example of something I still feel super *I-don't-fucking-know* about: In the play Eli and Matteo's dialogue is written in English, except when they're around Kat or Hanna. Hopefully it's clear that even though we're hearing their conversations in English, the characters are speaking Italian. But a few weeks ago, a friend sagely asked me . . . *Why* don't *they just speak Italian the whole time?* And my head exploded.

I keep thinking about this creative writing workshop I took during undergrad. I had submitted a chapter from a novel I was writing set in Florence—a place I've romanticized and ascribed so much meaning to. A place that, when I last visited five years ago, opened up bone-deep worlds of recognition inside me. A place I'm scared shitless to go back to.

The chapter had five, maybe six lines of Italian dialogue in it. My instructor—who was not Italian but had a (British) wife who had spent a few years racing horses in Italy or something—told me, a bit gleefully, that he had asked the wife to read my chapter and *she* said my Italian was "all wrong." Like. Grammatically. *Incorrecto.* Do not pass go, do not collect $200.

I'm sure the instructor gave me other, more useful feedback, but all I remember of that workshop is the shame burning in my gut.

In my dream world, you who's reading this happens to be a queer or trans person (or ally) who's fluent in Italian, and you also happen to be JAZZED about the art of translation, so you reach out to me and we collaborate to create a vision of this script that captures the characters' voices in Italian. And maybe even makes the characters' grasp of English more authentic as second-language speakers. And maybe along the way we become the best of friends, and possibly we trauma-bond over dead fathers and gender befuddlement, and eventually you visit me in the summertime in my new house with the fig tree out back that, just this morning, my mother reassured me, *Even you won't be able to kill.*

And if you who's reading this is *not* the translator/future collaborator of my dreams . . .

I hope there's still something here for you. I hope that this script has enough spaciousness and ambiguity—and also specificity—for you to bring your own lived experience to the page in a way that feels good. I hope you laugh a few big belly laughs. Or at least chuckle a little, to yourself, privately. If that's what tickles.

With love,
kai fig taddei
August 7th, 2022

Characters

ELI: Seventeen years old at the beginning of the play. Trans/gender-questioning. He is not out to his family in Italy.

MATTEO: Fourteen years old at the beginning of the play. Eli's brother. Cisgender.

KAT: Seventeen years old at the beginning of the play. Eli's cousin. Cisgender.

HANNA: Seventeen years old at the beginning of the play. Kat's best friend. Cisgender.

Setting

Toronto, Canada, and Florence, Italy.

Notes on the text

A forward slash (/) indicates overlapping dialogue.

The poem that Eli and Hanna recite on pages 54–56 is a combination of original writing and found poetry (roughly) translated from the Instagram poetry of Elia Bonci.

Act One

Prologue

ELI and KAT are on stage, together but separate. Dreamy lighting. ELI prays.

ELI: Benedicimi Padre per aver peccato.

Nel nome del Padre, del Figlio, e dello Spirito Santo, la mia ultima confessione è stata . . . tempo fa.

KAT: I'm sorry, I . . . I don't understand. My Italian's still not very . . .

ELI: Ho visto video pornografici.
Ho guidato ubriaca.
Ho mentito a mio fratello minore.
Ho baciato un ragazzo.
Ho odiato baciare un ragazzo.
Ho mentito a mio padre.
Ho mentito ai / miei amici.

KAT: Could you maybe speak a little slower, or—

ELI: Ho cercato l'assoluzione dai miei peccati da estranei su internet.
Ho ucciso un ragno quando avrei potuto risparmiargli la vita perché la gente / stava guardando.

KAT: What are you—

ELI: Mi sono toccata.
Mi sono toccata . . . spesso.
Ho fantasticato di avere un cazzo mentre mi / toccavo.

KAT: Eli, I don't—

ELI: Ho chiamato una ragazza con cui non ho mai parlato prima /
perché la gente ascoltava.

KAT: I can't—

ELI: Ho fantasticato di fare sesso con la ragazza che ho chiamato troia
perché forse lei avrebbe capito. Perché forse siamo uguali.

KAT: I DON'T UNDERSTAND!

ELI finally notices KAT.

A moment.

Fall

Scene One

*MATTEO enters, dressed as a gondolier. The costume looks like it's
maybe one size too small for him. He shovels a bowl of cereal into his
face and spills milk on himself.*

ELI enters.

MATTEO: Fuck!

ELI: Hey—watch it.

MATTEO: I spilled on my costume!

ELI: So?

MATTEO: *So*—I spilled on my costume!

ELI: No one will be able to tell.

MATTEO: Don't even have an oar . . .

ELI: Hmm?

MATTEO: I'm a gondolier. I should have an oar!

ELI: Don't have a gondola.

MATTEO: What kind of gondolier doesn't have an oar . . .

> *ELI grabs him and kisses him on his forehead and cheeks.*

ELI: You look beautiful. Okay? It'll be fun. Just relax.

MATTEO: I don't want to look *beautiful*.

ELI: Well, you're too pretty to be "handsome."

> *MATTEO hits ELI.*

What! It's not a bad thing. You look like Ultimo.

> *ELI tries to get MATTEO to dance with him, singing of few bars of Ultimo's "Il ballo delle incertezze."*

MATTEO: Ultimo's a fag.

ELI: Eh!

ELI clips MATTEO on the back of the head.

I said *watch it!*

MATTEO: What!

ELI: Don't say stuff like that. Seriously.

MATTEO: I don't see what the big deal is.

ELI: Aren't you going to be late for your party?

MATTEO: Yes. Aren't *you* going out?

ELI: No.

MATTEO: . . . It's Halloween.

ELI: So.

MATTEO: *so.* Aren't you going to go hang out? Drink? Be normal?

ELI: Halloween is an American holiday. I'll celebrate tomorrow. All Saints' Day.

MATTEO: What about Mass?

ELI: You really don't know anything.

MATTEO: I know you don't have any friends.

MATTEO shoves the half-empty bowl into ELI's hands.

Finish this!

ELI: I don't / want your—

MATTEO: BYEEEE, LOSER.

ELI: Yeah, yeah.

MATTEO exits.

ELI stands alone. He slurps the soggy remains of the cereal.

Scene Two

KAT and ELI are on opposite sides of the stage.

KAT is in Toronto; ELI is in Florence.

But they speak to each other like they're in the same room.

KAT is putting on makeup.

ELI is doing his nighttime routine: brushing his teeth, scrubbing his face, flossing.

ELI: I am sorry, you are a . . .

KAT: Satanist, yeah. But like! I'm not a *theistic* Satanist, which means you believe Satan is an actual *entity*, like a being with a physical form and stuff.

ELI: So you . . . do not think Satan is real?

KAT: No okay, so like I believe in a *symbolic* Satan.

ELI: A . . . sim-ball—?

KAT: A symbolic Satan, yeah, like. All the stuff Satan *represents*. Chaos, free will, gay shit. Cuz like—think about how powerful symbols are, right? Like, symbols have real power. I mean—the swastika, right? Powerful.

ELI: . . .

KAT: But I mean before the Nazis stole it the swastika was already like a super powerful Hindu symbol, right? Or. I think it was Hindu. Maybe like . . . Native American? Anyway, it was a symbol that had already been used by people for like thousands of years, so the Nazis basically just co-opted all that ancient power for themselves and so, yeah, I'm not an atheist, cuz I believe in spirituality and spell-casting and the afterlife, and I'm not a Christian because let's be honest, the Bible is fake news—

ELI: I am sorry, you think the / Bible is—?

KAT: I guess I'm like basically making up my own version of Satanism, right, which *incorporates* pagan traditions but isn't itself pagan or Wicca or whatever. It's something new. It's kind of, like. A non-binary religion. Can I say that?

ELI: Kat, could / you please—

KAT: Plus—*plus*—if Satan *is* an actual entity with a physical form or whatever then she's *obviously* a woman, and she's probably bisexual. Like. She's definitely bisexual.

ELI: The Bible / describes—

KAT: But every single Satanic church—even the Satanic Temple, which is like *rah rah reproductive rights*—every single Satanic church was invented by a dude. Which just. Doesn't feel right.

Beat.

I think it's our generation's, like. Collective prophecy or something. Make new traditions out of old ones. Not totally start from scratch—I don't think I'm a new messiah or whatever—but . . . rebuild.

Beat.

And you're . . .

ELI & KAT: Catholic.

ELI: Yes.

KAT: Right.

Beat.

Like, no-name brand, or . . . ?

ELI: Excuse me?

KAT: Do you follow, like. A specific type of Catholicism?

ELI: Oh. Yes. Roman Catholic.

KAT: Okay so I know that has nothing to do with the Roman pantheon or anything, but I sort of wish it did. Y'know? They were still kinda witchy back then. Artemis and Athena, and . . . there's one other one . . .

ELI: But I am not from Rome. I live in—

KAT: Florence, of course, yeah yeah, I know! But if like, *Italians* still worshipped all those old gods, like those *reeeeally* old gods—Aphrodite! Artemis, Athena, Aphrodite. The *real* Holy Trinity, right?

Beat.

ELI: Florence and Rome are very different places. They both enjoy to say bad things about southerners, but other than that . . .

KAT: But like . . . in a lot of ways, the Roman pantheon was kinda ahead of its time, right? It was kinda feminist, almost. Other than how Zeus cheated on Hera all the time and all the incest and rape and everything.

ELI: I think you are talking about the Greek pantheon?

KAT: Same gods, different names. Too bad they didn't have copyright laws back then, the Greeks could have patented the shit out of all their mythology. Wait. Can you patent religious beliefs?

ELI: I . . . do not know.

Beat.

KAT: I . . . hope this isn't weird.

ELI: . . . talking about religion?

KAT: No, just . . . talking. With me. I hope it's not weird. I felt sort of like a stalker, tracking down your Instagram account. I thought . . . I thought it would be good. If we knew each other. Sort of . . . normal. Most people know their cousins, right?

ELI: Right.

KAT: And then, when we started messaging, and you told me you were transgender, it was like . . . wow! I thought my dad was the only queer in the family. The only out queer, anyways. Which, okay, some people would say like: why do you need more than that? Isn't your dads being gay enough gay in your life? But it's different. They're my *dads*, and they're, like, men—old, *cis*gendered men.

    Beat.

ELI: Does your school finish very early? What time is it—

KAT: Three-thirty, yeah, but I have a spare last block so I came home early. The Wi-Fi is way too shitty at school to FaceTime. What time is it in Florence?

ELI: Nine-thirty.

KAT: Wait wait wait. This always fucks me up. Are you—

ELI: Ahead.

KAT: So, like. It's tomorrow there? Where you are?

ELI: Yes?

KAT: Or, well, I guess it's yesterday here.

ELI: The 31st.

KAT: Right. Wait. No. It's the 31st here, too. Halloween.

ELI: Yes.

    Beat.

KAT: Wait. But you're wearing pajamas! Why aren't you out?? Ohmygod it's HALLOWEEN in ITALY and you just BRUSHED YOUR TEETH?

ELI: My dad is in Rome again, on business. I, uh . . . need to . . . care for Matteo.

KAT: Ohhh, shit. Sorry. Babysitting on Halloween. That fucking sucks.

ELI: Yes.

> Beat. ELI *debates whether or not to tell* KAT *this next piece of information.*

I think he might have a girlfriend there?

KAT: Who, Matteo? Oh, wait, like—your dad? In Rome?

ELI: I have heard him on the phone with her. He has not dated anyone since . . . I do not know if I should tell Matteo.

KAT: Matteo must be like, what now, twelve?

ELI: Fourteen.

KAT: Holy shit. No WAY. Fourteen?

ELI: Fourteen, yes.

KAT: No way!

ELI: His birthday was last—

KAT: Oh yeah, totally, totally, saw your post. Scorpio.

> Beat.

ELI: What . . . ?

KAT: He's a Scorpio.

Beat.

Or a Libra. Anyways, he should probably know, don't you think? That your dad's dating again? Like . . . if you're dad's serious about this girlfriend, there's not much you can do. Matteo's gonna find out.

ELI: Matteo is . . . sensitive.

KAT: Mmmmm. Scorpio for sure.

Beat.

Hey, I've been learning Italian!

ELI: Stai prendendo lezioni?

KAT: . . . Huh?

ELI: I thought you . . . I asked if you were taking classes.

KAT: Oh. No! I'm self-teaching. Duolingo. There's no option to take Italian in school, only French or Spanish. I guess I *could* take Spanish. They're like, basically the same language, right? Grammatically or whatever?

HANNA enters.

(to HANNA) Seriously? Why can't you be chronically late like everybody else!

HANNA: Santiago was going on and on about Doug Ford and I couldn't take it anymore, so I told him you were having a panic attack and needed me to come take care of you but then he *insisted* on driving me here and—oh! Sorry.

KAT: It's cool. This is my cousin, Eli. Our dads are brothers. This is my best friend, Hanna.

> ELI *waves.* HANNA *waves back. It's awkward. Maybe somebody's video freezes. A few moments here.*

HANNA: Are you in—?

KAT: He's the one I told you about, yeah.

ELI: Florence.

HANNA: Wow. *Florence.*

ELI: It is really not so impressive.

HANNA: But *Italy* . . .

ELI: If you were here . . .

KAT: He's the one I told you about! The trans one!

> *A beat.*

Oh, shit, sorry—did I—did I fuck up?

ELI: No, it is all right . . .

KAT: I just—I was so excited to find out there was another queer in the family! Somebody like, the same age as me! All my cousins are still babies, they haven't had time to deconstruct the patriarchy yet. And Hanna's a safe person, I swear. She's probably the safest person

I know. And, like—I guess I think about what my dad went through, with our grandpa, back in Italy . . . the mandatory military service, getting kicked out, moving to a different country . . . I know it was the seventies and things are probably super different now, but like. He wasn't even trans.

HANNA: *(to ELI)* That must be really difficult.

> *ELI shrugs.*

KAT: I keep telling him he needs to come visit for Pride next summer!

ELI: I do not know how I would pay for—

KAT: There's loads of time to save up money, buy a ticket really early, you can get like HUGE discounts if you buy early enough—

HANNA: Have you ever been to Canada?

ELI: Never. No.

HANNA: You're not missing out on much anyway. I mean, you live in *Italy* . . .

KAT: Don't tell him that! He's not gonna come if you tell / him *that*—

HANNA: I've only ever visited Italy once—I was pretty little though. We went to Venice, Florence, Milan, and Rome. Venice was my favourite. All those waterways. We went on a ride in one of those long boats, what are they called . . .

ELI: Gondolas.

> *KAT exits.*

HANNA: Yeah! It was September—I remember, cuz I started school late that year and I had all these assignments and things I had to catch up on when we got home, I was so stressed—but not at the time. At the time, it was perfect. All those little archways, and the opera house, and the statues of winged lions and . . . so, you're really not missing much. Toronto, we have snow. And the CN Tower. And the Tories, apparently. Lake Ontario's so big you could pretend it's the ocean, I guess, but it doesn't smell the same.

ELI: Like hot garbage.

HANNA laughs.

HANNA: Some days, sure—Wednesdays, that's garbage day where we live—but not *all* of / Toronto—

ELI: No, Venice. That is what it smells like, now. Like garbage, left to rot out in the sun. It is a city full of ghosts, all year, until the summer. And then the tourists come. But this is a real problem. Most of the year, there is no one. No one to look after the city as it . . .

He searches for the word, but can't find it, so gestures "sinks."

It is a real problem. Everyone is gone.

Beat. KAT re-enters.

KAT: Heyyy, sorry to abandon you so quickly, Eli, but since *someone* doesn't understand the concept of being fashionably late, I should probably run. We'll talk soon though, yeah?

ELI: That would be nice.

HANNA: Great to meet you!

ELI: You, too.

KAT: CIAO CIAOOO!

> *KAT blows kisses at ELI.*

> *ELI opens a trap door in the floor and takes out a number of white candles.*

> *He sings quietly to himself while he lights a few of the candles and places them along the lip of the stage.*

Scene Three

> *KAT's bedroom.*

KAT: I don't think it's crazy.

HANNA: Not *crazy*, but—

KAT: What? People crowdfund for less important things all the time. To make video games, web comics, fanfiction, all kinds of shit—

HANNA: Shouldn't we ask him?

KAT: —bored, rich kids crowdfund so they can spend other people's money on things to do so they aren't so fucking bored all the time!

HANNA: Yeah . . .

> *ELI starts painting his face in male drag.*

KAT: Think about it. He comes here, he crashes with you and your mom—

HANNA: Wait, what?

KAT: —he gets to see what it's like in Canada. He wants to come here for post-secondary. You know in Italy it's legal to discriminate against people based on their gender.

HANNA: It's not like Italy's a Third World country, though.

KAT: *Developing* country.

HANNA: Okay, so it's not like it's a *developing* country. It's in the West, it's—

KAT: Ummm, news flash: being a Western country doesn't automatically make it, like, utopia.

HANNA: Okay, but a second ago you were talking about *Canada* as if we hadn't like genocided thousands and thousands of / people—

KAT: PLUS, if Eli moved here for school and got his citizenship, he could get his hormones covered and everything. There's no way they cover medical stuff in Italy.

HANNA: Wait, wait. Are you even sure he wants to be on hormones? I thought you said he was pretty new to all this stuff? Like, still confused?

KAT: Last time I checked, *you* weren't head of the GSA.

HANNA: It just . . . it seems like you're making a lot of assumptions.

KAT: Umm. He's my *cugino*!

> *KAT's accent is horrible. You don't have to be a native Italian speaker to hear it.*

HANNA: I'm sorry?

KAT: That means "cousin." In Italian. He's *my* cousin.

HANNA: I mean. Sort of.

Beat.

KAT: What do you mean, "sort of?"

HANNA: Kat, I'm sorry, okay, it just feels like—

KAT: No, what do you mean, *sort of?*

HANNA: I'm just saying, you've never even met him in real life. Or your uncle. My cousins and I grew up together. They can pretty much read my mind. I just don't think it's the same.

KAT: Yeah well, my dad didn't exactly leave Italy on good terms with everyone. It's not like I *chose* to be estranged from—

HANNA: But see, that's my point! Don't you think bringing Eli here might, I don't know . . . open up old wounds?

KAT: That's *my* point! If my dad's own *brother* wouldn't accept him being *gay*, how do you think he's going to feel about his *kid* being *trans?*

HANNA: Maybe he's changed.

Pause.

KAT: So. Your mom would let Eli stay with you guys, right?

HANNA: I mean, I'd have to talk to her but yeah / like, probably—

KAT: Social workers *live* for this kind of thing. Right? Your mom is the best. She's so chill.

HANNA: I mean yeah, she is pretty progressive . . .

KAT: UGH. I wish she was *my* mom. Not that there's anything wrong with having two dads, you know I love my dads, but they're so uptight about everything. I'm hungry—leftovers?

HANNA: I'd eat. Is it okay if I stay here, though? I want to finish up some chem homework before the party.

KAT: Do your thing.

> *KAT exits.*

> *ELI has finished painting his face in male drag. He looks across the stage and locks eyes with HANNA. They wave, again. It is significantly less awkward than the last time.*

Scene Four

> *MATTEO enters. It is later the same night. He is drunk.*

MATTEO: Who are you supposed to be?

ELI: . . . Pavarotti.

> *Beat.*

(singing) 'O sole, 'o sole mio
Sta 'nfronte a te!
Sta 'nfronte a te!

MATTEO: Shhhh! Shut up shut up!

ELI: Are you drunk?

MATTEO: Why did you dress up if you aren't going out? Loser.

ELI: I hung out with some new friends, actually. Online.

MATTEO: Who—a bunch of creepy old men pretending to be teenage girls? You must fit right in!

ELI puts MATTEO in a headlock.

Get off get off get off me!

ELI lets go.

ELI: Did you have fun?

MATTEO: Everyone was dressed up like devils and angels, witches and vampires.

ELI: So you stood out.

MATTEO: Giorgio stole my hat.

ELI: Screw Giorgio.

MATTEO: We played spin the bottle.

ELI: Kids still play that game?

MATTEO: It was humiliating. I had to kiss Niccolo.

ELI: Niccolo? Like the one you're always bringing over to study?

MATTEO: I want to die.

ELI: He's cute!

MATTEO: Maybe to you.

> *A beat.*

ELI: Matteo, listen . . .

MATTEO: I'm such a fucking idiot . . .

ELI: If the rest of the kids at that party were half as drunk as you, no one will remember come / Monday—

MATTEO: Alessandro had his phone out.

ELI: What? Why?

> *Beat.*

Let me tell you something. Are you listening? *Eh—are you listening?*

MATTEO: Yes, yes.

ELI: Okay. Listen carefully.

> *Beat.*

Girls like a feminine boy.

MATTEO: Pffff.

ELI: It's about power. Alessandro, he has power, he pretends that he's confident, he pretends that he does what he does because he can but that's not really the answer. Now, why do you think he wanted to film two boys kissing?

MATTEO shrugs.

Because when he gets home, he's going to watch that video, and he's going to . . .

ELI mimes jerking off, groaning. MATTEO is horrified.

ELI nods, sagely.

Girls like a boy who isn't afraid to kiss another boy. It means he's secure in his masculinity, that he knows he doesn't need to do all this posturing and clucking about like a rooster to get their attention. Alessandro filmed you and Niccolo because he wished it was him. He wished he could be you, in that moment. He wished he could inhabit you and Niccolo both, or maybe wished to be sandwiched in the middle of you, one on each cheek.

ELI grabs MATTEO and plants two wet, sloppy kisses on his cheeks. MATTEO pulls away.

MATTEO: You're insane.

ELI unties the kerchief from MATTEO's neck and ties it around his own neck.

ELI: I bet you didn't know, little brother, that the tradition of the gondolier has been around for nine hundred years. As long as our family has been in Tuscany. But in all that time: no women allowed! Fathers would pass down their knowledge, their boats, the gondolier-ing life, to their sons, only their sons. No female gondoliers. Until one day, finally, it happens: a woman gondolier, out on the water!

MATTEO: Have you been reading dad's dumb magazines?

ELI: But then, that female gondolier— the only one ever in the history of Venice? She comes out as a transgender man. So maybe there hasn't ever been a female gondolier. Has there?

Beat. ELI and MATTEO stare at one another.

MATTEO: I'm going to bed.

MATTEO exits.

HANNA enters.

The following conversation takes place over Instagram messages, but we hear it as though HANNA and ELI are in the same room.

HANNA: Hey.

ELI: Hey.

HANNA: I just wanted to say, I've been reading some of your poetry, and I think it's really good. I mean, I'm sure I'm not reading it exactly as it's *meant* to be read, because Instagram translates it from Italian to English and well, I'm sure there's some stuff, like, some connotative stuff and maybe subtext and nuance that it totally misses but the images at the centre of it all, like the *heart* of it . . . I think the images are beautiful.

ELI: . . . Grazie.

An awkward beat.

HANNA: What year of high school are you in?

ELI: My final. The end.

HANNA: Cool. Kat said high school in Italy is different than high school here.

ELI: Yes. I tried to explain it to her, but . . .

HANNA: She steamrolled you?

ELI: "Steamrolled"?

HANNA: Oh, that's like . . . when someone . . . controls the conversation. Maybe . . . interrupts you? Maybe . . . doesn't hear what you're saying?

ELI: Ah. Yes. She "steamrolls" me.

HANNA: Try not to take it too personally. She steamrolls me, too, and I'm her best friend. She means well, but she's . . . excitable.

> *Beat.*

So, how does it work? High school in Italy.

ELI: I do not think it is interesting.

HANNA: Try me.

ELI: Every high school has a different . . . subject. Mine, we study . . . psychology . . . philosophy . . . similar subjects. But there are also high schools for science and math, or for how to become an artist.

HANNA: So, like . . . you have to pick a career—like commit to what you want to do way, way in the future—right when you start high school? I don't know if I could have handled that. I don't know if I could handle that *now*.

Beat.

How did you know?

ELI: Know . . . ?

HANNA: Which high school you wanted to go to.

ELI: I am interested in people. Why do people . . . do these actions, or . . .

HANNA: So do you want to be a psychologist?

ELI: Maybe.

HANNA: Why didn't you pick art? I mean, since you write poetry and everything, I would have thought . . .

Beat.

ELI: I did, to begin. I began grade nine in a *liceo artistico*—a, eh, school for the arts. But then, I, ah . . . I changed.

Beat.

I had a . . . I was . . . sad. I don't know how to say it in English. I was really, really . . . sad. And then I became interested in why, why am I so sad, and I switched schools.

HANNA: Oh. Well. Thanks for . . . thank you for sharing that with me.

ELI: . . . But I don't know anything about you! Except, I see, ahhh— dog! You have a dog?

KAT enters carrying two large, heavy plastic garbage bags.

KAT: Okay, so it is a *labyrinth* down there. Like . . . in *Labyrinth*.

HANNA: Huh?

KAT: David Bowie? Whatever. I mean, I knew my dads' hoarding had gotten worse, but it is out of control bad. Apparently we have two deep freezes full of meat down there. TWO DEEP FREEZES. And I opened one up and maybe it's cuz it's Halloween but like I was half expecting it to be full of bodies, chopped up and vacuum sealed.

HANNA: Isn't the whole "queer psychopath" trope a bit tired?

KAT: For all we know, there COULD be bodies down there. It's that bad. But, I suppose, that's at least to our advantage when it comes to . . . this!

> *KAT dumps out the two enormous bags and the contents spill across the stage: colourful boas, dark cloaks, masks, maybe a few offensive/appropriative costumes ordered off Amazon in the early 2010s. She starts rummaging through the heaps.*

ELI: *(over Instagram)* You still there?

HANNA: *(over Instagram)* Yeah, I am. Kat just got back.

KAT: Get off your phone and help me!

> *Beat.*

Ugh. I sound like our teachers. Remember that documentary they made us watch, what, last year? "Increased exposure to screen time in our children may be to blame for the decrease in blah blah fucking blah."

> *KAT looks up—HANNA is still on her phone, smiling to herself.*

Hey. Am I talking to myself here?

HANNA: Sorry, sorry.

KAT: What's going on.

HANNA: What do you mean?

KAT: You have a stupid smile on your face. Who are you messaging?

HANNA: No one . . .

KAT: Don't lie to me! I just put a book of hexes on hold from the library.

HANNA: What do you want to be? Wait. Let me guess. Sexy witch? Am I wrong?

KAT: Am *I* wrong? You're flirting! *That* is your flirting face! It might be less obvious when you're sober, but I can still spot it. Who is he?

HANNA: How heteronormative of you.

KAT: Oh, come on. We both know there's only room for one massive queer in this relationship. Spill.

> *HANNA finds a* Scream *mask in the pile. She puts it on and starts creeping towards KAT. KAT turns around and notices her.*

. . . Take it off. Using my phobia against me to distract me is not going to . . . Take that off RIGHT NOW. Hanna. Ohmygod I'm going to kill you, DON'T EVEN THINK ABOUT THIS IS SO NOT FUNNY FUCK YOU FUCK YOU FUCK YOU.

> *HANNA chases KAT.*

Perhaps there is some silly business here, running in circles, etc., before HANNA *chases* KAT *off stage, screaming.*

Shift.

ELI *approaches the costume pile.*

He dresses himself.

What he wears is up to the performer.

KAT *runs back on stage, dives into the costume pile, and hides herself beneath a mountain of costumes.*

HANNA *re-enters, panting, and looks around for* KAT—*but instead sees* ELI.

He approaches her, takes the Scream *mask off her face.*

They dance.

MATTEO *enters in his gondolier costume, fancier now, rowing a gondola.*

He gestures to HANNA *and* ELI *to get in, and they clamber into the gondola.* MATTEO *rows them off stage.*

KAT *re-emerges from the costume pile.*

Hanna? You are dead to me, you are so dead to me. HANNA. Where are you hiding?

HANNA re-enters.

HANNA: Sorry, sorry. I peed myself laughing, I had to go to the bathroom and rinse my underwear out.

Beat.

Seriously!

KAT: Karma.

HANNA: I love you.

KAT: Go to hell.

HANNA picks an elaborate witch's hat out of the costume pile.

HANNA: How about this?

KAT: What happened to *sexy* witch.

HANNA: You don't think this is sexy?

KAT: I want to be, like. Sarah Jessica Parker in *Hocus Pocus*. Okay?

HANNA: Kat, please just assume I'm not going to understand your obscure movie references.

KAT: *Hocus Pocus* is not "obscure"!

HANNA: What are you, a baby boomer?

KAT: Gasp!

HANNA: Maybe that's what I should dress up as for Halloween. Go around the party tomorrow denying climate change.

KAT: Spooky.

Scene Five

Morning of the next day (November 1st) in Florence—VERY early morning in Toronto.

ELI enters carrying a large bouquet of flowers. MATTEO slumps along behind him.

MATTEO: I think I'm going to puke.

ELI: As long as you don't do it during the Eucharist.

MATTEO: Oh, no. I can't drink wine right now. I can't even *smell* wine right now. I can't even *think* about smelling wine right now. I'm going to vomit all over the priest.

ELI: It's watered down, you big baby.

MATTEO: Stupid Mass. Stupid fasting.

ELI: I tried to wake you up earlier to at least eat something, but you wouldn't / budge.

MATTEO: My head . . .

ELI: By the time we get through all the rites and readings, you'll be good as new. Peter 4:3: "you have spent enough time in the past doing what pagans choose to do—living in debauchery, lust, drunkenness, orgies, / carousing and—"

MATTEO: *Orgies?*

ELI: Yes, little brother. I'm sorry to be the bearer of bad news. The Bible is strictly anti-orgy. I guess Alessandro's going to have to give up that dream of his, of a threesome with you and Niccolo, all of you / locked together in joyful—

MATTEO: Shut up shut up! Pervert!

They jostle one another.

If I puke, it's your fault.

HANNA and KAT enter. KAT is dressed as a witch; she wears a Gothic silver cross around her neck. HANNA is dressed as a mad scientist.

KAT: Humour me, bitch!

HANNA: I'm tired . . .

KAT: You can sleep when you're dead! It's All Hallows Day! The astronomical midpoint between the fall equinox and the winter solstice! A *thousand-year-old* pagan festival! It's MAGIC TIME.

HANNA: Can't "magic time" wait until tomorrow?

KAT: Do you *see* that full moon?

HANNA: I'm pretty sure it's waxing. Or . . . waning? Which is which . . .

ELI: *(over Instagram)* Still awake?

HANNA: *(over Instagram)* Ohhhhh yeah. For better or worse.

ELI: *(over Instagram)* Having a good night?

HANNA: *(over Instagram)* Mostly. Except that Kat is going full-blown *Sabrina the Teenage Witch* on me.

MATTEO: *(to ELI)* "No cellphones in church!"

MATTEO snatches ELI's phone out of his hands.

ELI and MATTEO go through the motions of Mass. MATTEO is doing his best not to throw up everywhere.

KAT: I want to build an altar.

HANNA: Kat.

KAT: All we need are some spices, dried leaves, small bones, we already have / plenty of wine—

HANNA: *Kat.* Please . . .

KAT: —and grave rubbings. The cemetery is on our way back to your house anyway, so I figured we could stop there on our way. I brought charcoal.

HANNA: Are you out of your mind? Do you *want* to get mugged?

KAT: I thought we could ask for a blessing. From the spirits. Or, like, Diana.

HANNA: Why would you ask for a blessing from Ben's mom.

KAT: Ohmygod not *that*—Diana, like, big-dyke-energy, goddess of the moon and the hunt? Keep up!

HANNA: Don't you have to give gifts to that kind of god? Like . . . old-timey gods?

KAT: Ya, sure! Ooo. Ya. Good idea. Ya. A gift. So let's do the grave rubbing first, and then find something we can offer up / as like—

HANNA: There will be police out, it's 1:30 / on Halloween, there will be cops everywhere—

KAT: This is the best time of year to commune with spirits!

HANNA: Are you gonna start claiming to be a prophet next?

KAT: WHY DOES EVERYONE—no! It is Halloween and I'm sad and I'm fucked up and the world is burning and I just want to build an altar with my best friend. Okay? Is that so weird?

HANNA: Yes. It is.

>   *Beat. HANNA sighs.*

But okay. Okay!

KAT: Eeee! I love you.

>   *ELI and MATTEO are finishing up Mass.*
>
>   *The stage becomes a graveyard.*
>
>   *On one side, KAT and HANNA begin the process of grave rubbing.*
>
>   *On the other, ELI and MATTEO gather around the grave of ELI and MATTEO's mother.*

ELI: Eterno riposo, dona a loro, o Signore,
e splenda ad essi la luce perpetua.
Riposino in pace.

MATTEO & ELI: Amen.

>   *A silence. ELI places the flowers to rest on his mother's grave.*

MATTEO vomits, violently. All over the grave.

KAT and HANNA finish up their grave rubbing at the cemetery and stumble back to KAT's home, collecting fallen leaves and acorns on their way. They stop along the lip of the stage, where ELI lit candles earlier in the play, and begin to build their altar. We are now in KAT's bedroom.

HANNA: What should we offer up?

KAT: What sorts of things do you think Diana would like?

HANNA: To Google!

HANNA googles.

ThoughtCo.com says that it depends on the god. That you've got to "personalize your offering."

KAT: Like how Instagram always gives me targeted ads for super cute, recycled clothes? Like that sweater that says

HANNA & KAT: "Plant more trees, save the bees, clean the seas!"

KAT: I would totally do someone favors if they paid me in cute clothes.

HANNA: Yeah, exactly. So, like . . . common gifts for gods of nature and prosperity are like . . . milk, beer, bread?

KAT: We drank all the beer . . .

HANNA: In pagan times, they'd have temples, so they'd leave offerings out in the forest to be eaten by wildlife.

KAT: We can't litter, though. And there isn't exactly any wildlife in Toronto.

HANNA: Raccoons?

Beat.

Ummm, okay . . . it says you can burn herbs, too. Do you have any catnip?

KAT: We can burn *catnip?*

HANNA: It says here: "first mentioned in the eleventh century hexameter poem, *De viribus herbarum*—"

KAT: Wow, what a romantic subject for a poem—

HANNA: "— catnip was prized by Native American tribes such as the Cherokee, Hoh, Delaware and Iroquois, as well as by Europeans for its ability to calm the nerves and support a deep sleep."

KAT: Huh. Sounds legit. I'll grab some!

> *KAT goes to get catnip. She comes back, and they prep the altar. They light the white candle and burn the catnip. Smoke curls upwards.*

Waitwaitwait. Is this gonna get us high?

HANNA: No.

KAT: Oh.

HANNA: Shouldn't you like . . . say some words? For the blessing? Offering? Whatever?

Beat. KAT *thinks.*

KAT: Did I ever tell you about my dream?

HANNA: Oh, yes, of course. Your dream!

KAT: Are you messing with me?

HANNA: No, you were so specific! How could I forget that one dream you had—

KAT: Okay, okay, I get it. Be serious for a second.

Beat.

It was why I reached out to Eli. He showed up in my dreams one night. Probably the first time a boy has ever showed up in my dreams in, like, not a sexy way.

HANNA: I should *hope* it wasn't sexual.

KAT: I hadn't even heard Eli speak at this point—I'd only just found him on Instagram, so I barely knew what he *looked* like—but he shows up in my dream and starts speaking Italian to me.

HANNA: How did you know it was Italian?

KAT: Because he's Italian.

HANNA: But you don't speak Italian

KAT: I'm learning!

HANNA: So you understood him?

KAT: No, but I *knew* it was Italian, okay? He's reciting this Italian, and it's beautiful, and we're like . . . suspended in the air. In space. And behind him there's these planets, or stars, I don't know—

HANNA: Giant balls of gas—

KAT: —these giant balls of gas yeah, and they're, like, exploding. Behind him and all around us, it's like . . . like we're standing in the middle of the big bang. The universe is giving birth all around us. And then all of a sudden, he's walking away, forwards, past me, and there are little sparks, like these little comets coming out of his heels as he walks away and then . . .

Beat.

HANNA: And then . . . ?

KAT: And then I woke up and found him on Instagram.

Suddenly, one of the candles topples over.

KAT: OHMYGODWHATTHEHELL   **HANNA:** Ahhh!

HANNA: What was that?

KAT: I don't know!

HANNA: Was that like a positive sign or—?

KAT: I don't know I don't know!

HANNA: I thought you made up the rules!

KAT: I didn't make that happen!

HANNA: Well can't you, I dunno, interpret it or something?

KAT: No! Google!

HANNA returns, once again, to the shrine of Google.

HANNA: Ummm, okay, so it says: "When a candle topples over or the flame self-extinguishes, it means your work has ended and your prayer was received."

KAT: Okay. That sounds good!

HANNA: "It can also indicate that your spell has been opposed by the spirit realm . . ."

Beat.

KAT: Let's go with the first one.

Scene Six

Three days later: November 4th.

ELI and HANNA are on FaceTime.

HANNA: That's so awful. On your mother's *grave*?

ELI makes an upchucking gesture. HANNA laughs.

I'm so sorry, I shouldn't be laughing, it's not funny—

ELI: It was pretty funny.

Beat.

I feel you know more things of me than I know of you. Ummm. You
have a little brother who does the . . .

HANNA: Saxophone. Badly.

ELI: And a . . . golden retriever?

HANNA: Yeah. Shaggy.

> *Beat.*

It's a bad joke. My brother named him. We used to have another dog,
too—a Great Dane—we got them at the same time, so my brother
named them Scooby-Doo and Shaggy. It was his all-time favourite
TV show.

> *Beat.*

Y'know. *Scooby-Doo?* The cartoon?

> *ELI shakes his head.*

Oh, okay. Ummm. it's a cartoon, like for little kids. But in the cartoon,
Scooby-Doo is a dog, and Shaggy is a person, soooo now that Scooby-Doo is dead Shaggy's name makes even less sense.

ELI: I'm sorry. About . . . "Scoody Boo."

> *Beat.*

HANNA: That's okay. Great Danes don't live long. Their hearts are
too big.

> *Beat.*

ELI: I know . . . you play football, you are, uh, / *il difensore*?

HANNA: Defence! Yeah. We call it soccer here, though. Football is a whole other thing. Your team is famous for its defence.

ELI: Ahh, yes yes, *catenaccio*. We used to play very much with the defence. But since a while, we play more aggressively. Do you see the World Cup?

HANNA: I've watched it every year since I was, like, four? My dad is obsessed. I remember—I think it was, like, 2006? —the finals, France versus Italy—

ELI: Zidane and Materazzi!

    ELI mimes head-butting someone.

HANNA: Yeah, yeah!! Holy shit, the toxic masculinity was off the CHARTS.

ELI: Okay, okay, but no more football. Too much about football in Italy. Let us return to you.

HANNA: If you want . . .

ELI: You will save the fishes!

    HANNA laughs.

HANNA: Yeah, I mean, I wanna study marine biology. But the thing is there's like, no jobs. I'll probably just end up getting a degree in biochem and working in a lab trying to cure cancer or something. Because that's where all the money is.

    Beat.

Not that, like—I'm not saying curing cancer is a bad thing! *But* . . . if life in the oceans dies out, there will have been no point in curing cancer. There will be no more cancer, because there will be no more people. Or, if there are, they'll have more urgent stuff to worry about.

ELI: Like?

HANNA: I don't know, like . . . constant climate catastrophe resulting in mass displacement and starvation and disease and ultimately, extinction.

Beat.

ELI: Do you believe in God?

HANNA: That's a loaded question.

ELI: I'm only curious.

HANNA: Do you? Believe in God.

ELI: Yes.

HANNA: And . . . it doesn't bother you, the way Pope Francis talks / about—

ELI: The Pope is not the Church. The people are the Church. And the Pope *definitely* is not God.

KAT enters.

KAT: SURPRISE. You're not the only one who can be fashionably early.

HANNA quickly hangs up on ELI.

HANNA: You've never been early a day in your life. What's going on?

KAT: I did it.

HANNA: What? *What?*

>   *Beat.*

Ohmygod . . . like, *"it"* it?! With who??

KAT: Mind out of the gutter, woman! Are you ovulating?

>   *HANNA's phone vibrates.*

HANNA: I don't know . . .

ELI: Are you okay?

KAT: What do you mean you don't know?! There's like a million apps for that! Hanna, it's important to be in touch with your cycle.

HANNA: Thanks, Mom.

>   *KAT flops next to HANNA and opens her laptop.*

KAT: I launched it!

HANNA: You launched . . . ? *(realization)* The crowdfunding campaign . . .

KAT: This morning. And, you *would not believe this—*

HANNA: —did you talk to / him first?

KAT: —we've already raised TWENTY PERCENT OF OUR FUNDRAISING GOAL. In one day! Isn't that abso-fucking-lutely ri-diculous?

HANNA: I mean, yeah . . . it's pretty unbelievable—

KAT: This like, B-list non-binary actor—I think they were a guest star on *Law and Order* or something—anyways, they reposted it on Twitter, and it totally blew up, and / now—

HANNA: Did you talk to Eli?

KAT: No? I'm going to wait until we reach our fundraising goal. Then I'll tag him in a post on Instagram. Man, this is probably like the nicest thing I've ever done for anyone. And I'm, like. *Really* nice.

HANNA: Kat . . .

KAT: *Ha-nna!*

HANNA: Look, I totally get that you're excited, and I'm sure that . . . if you *warn* him . . . Eli will be excited, too. But I really think it's important you at least shoot him a message, you know, to ask if—

KAT: Waitwaitwait. I just got another email. "Congratulations! Anonymous has donated A HUNDRED DOLLARS to your campaign!" Seriously, can you believe this? I can't believe it. I mean. I guess I can believe it. Because globalization, right? Like, half the people who've donated to the campaign, I don't even know them. But they read Eli's story and they *felt* something. It spoke to them.

HANNA: *(reading)* Since when is Eli an orphan?

KAT: He's, like. Half an orphan.

HANNA: . . . "baptized by hate and intolerance, he was robbed of the opportunity to connect to his truest, most authentic self" . . . did he like, tell you this stuff?

KAT: Donations coming in from the United States, lots of small ones from Toronto—get this, *Matt* donated.

HANNA: Um. Duh.

KAT: Only ten bucks but like ten bucks, that's an hour of your life when you work at McDonald's.

HANNA: Matt has a boner for you.

KAT: Can't a teenage boy ever just do something to benefit humanity?

HANNA: Not if it doesn't also benefit his dick.

KAT: Sexist.

HANNA: I think you mean "androphobic."

KAT: This is bringing people together!

HANNA: Like you and Matt?

KAT: You know I'm off boys. I have another date next week with that gender studies major.

HANNA: Isn't she like twenty?

KAT: Whatever. So, depending on how *that* goes . . . you might get to freak out properly about me losing my V-card.

Beat.

Honestly, aren't you at all interested in sex? The dirty deed? Coitus?

KAT: Please stop talking.

KAT: Boning? Buggering? Bumping uglies—

HANNA: Stop.

KAT: Some good old candling?

HANNA: What the hell is candling?

KAT: Like, fingering, but instead you use—

HANNA: You need to spend one hundred percent less time on the Internet.

KAT: Maybe *you* need to spend less time on the Internet . . . flirting with *strangers*.

HANNA: What?

KAT: Don't think I've forgotten about that boy you were messaging.

HANNA: Oh . . . about that . . .

KAT: Ohmygod. Slut! You hypocritical *slut*!

HANNA: It's Eli.

    Beat.

KAT: . . . What?

HANNA: Eli? Your cousin? He's the cute boy I've been messaging.

KAT: But you're . . .

HANNA makes a "yes?" gesture.

You're like the straightest person I know.

HANNA: How am I the "straightest person / you know"?

KAT: I don't know, you like—wear sports jerseys just because. You cried when you cut an inch off your hair. You like, genuinely enjoy *The Office*. Plus, news flash: you've only ever dated boys. Your only crushes have been boys! I guess I'm just a bit, like. Surprised.

HANNA: Okay, this is like, deeply ironic coming from you? You do realize that?

Beat.

KAT: I'm just . . . surprised. That's all. I'm processing. Gimme a second.

Beat.

Okay. I've processed. I approve.

HANNA: Wow, thank god, what would I have done if I didn't have your blessing . . .

KAT: . . . That was sarcasm. You're never sarcastic. I didn't even know you were capable of sarcasm.

Beat.

You *really* like him. What's the word for when you're a slut but like. For romance.

HANNA: We barely know each other . . . we don't even live in the same country, but . . . we've been messaging for three days straight. Nonstop. And, honestly, I'm not even sure if he is a trans guy. I asked him if there were gender-neutral pronouns in Italian and like . . . you should have seen his face. He's so cute. And confused. And I'm confused. This is all really, really confusing. But honestly, even if he doesn't know what his gender is, I . . . don't think I care?

Beat.

KAT: You are so gonna fuck him.

HANNA: Okay sorry so YOU'RE ovulating?

KAT: Well if he's *staying* with you for Pride . . . how would that even work, though? Should we like, buy you a strap-on, or—

HANNA: I think you should have talked to him first. Before launching the crowdfunding campaign.

Beat.

KAT: Look, he's told me some of the shit he's been through, and I was like, Jesus man, how do you cope, and you know what he said?

HANNA shrugs.

He said: "I write poetry."

HANNA: . . . Okay?

KAT: He's never been to therapy, he's not part of a GSA, he literally admitted himself he has no friends—he's all alone over there! He doesn't know how to ask for help!

HANNA: Or maybe he doesn't *want* help . . .

KAT: Look I get that you're like two seconds into some kind of queer awakening but you don't actually know what it's like to *be* queer.

HANNA: I wasn't saying that—

KAT: The hardest thing you've ever had to live through was a divorce, and your parents still play online chess together! I'm doing a nice thing. Okay? Maybe you just don't get it because you've never stood out anywhere. You've literally never been on the outside. Everywhere you go, you blend in. Do you know how exhausting it is to be stared at all the time? On the TTC, in the grocery store, on my street—everywhere! I wish there was someone out there looking out for me like I'm looking out for Eli. Someone who was paying attention for the right reasons, not cuz of how I look or the stupid shit I say but like actually looking at me, like paying enough attention to realize that I'm too fucking tired for this shit, I don't want to have to ask for what I need all the time, okay, I don't want to have to express myself twenty-four-fucking-seven, sometimes I just want somebody who gets it to be like, hey, let me do this for you, I'm gonna do this for you now. That's who I'm trying to be for Eli. I'm trying to be, like. A bridge.

Beat.

Jesus. I seriously never thought a boy—or a girl—or whatever he is, I honestly don't care—I never thought some stupid crush would make you act like this, and it's fucking annoying. You're being super annoying, okay? I'm annoyed that we even have to like, have this conversation right now. Fuck.

Pause.

HANNA: I still don't get why you won't just ask him what he wants.

KAT's phone vibrates.

ELI: Kat, Hanna disappeared in the middle of a call and I'm worried about her. Do you know is she safe?

KAT: Wow. Just . . . wow.

KAT exits.

Shift.

Time passes.

Some movement here.

Maybe we see the numbers for the crowdfunding campaign creeping steadily upwards.

ELI: I feel scared to tell you this, but . . . I wrote something for you. Maybe . . . I should wait?

HANNA: You wrote something for me?

ELI: I tried to write it in English, but the words ran away from me, in all directions.

ELI has put the poem, originally written in Italian, through Google Translate.

The Italian words spill across the stage all around them.

I saw you in so many ways, maybe something like

HANNA: two hundred thousand   ELI: duecentomila

ELI: I'm a supernova
My cosmos, you
The mouth shaped like a planet

ELI & HANNA: I escaped from my land, from my everyday life

HANNA: I escaped like a thief in a dark night
And I fell to the peak
Like a star in San Marino

ELI & HANNA: Like a leaf in the fall

ELI: I am in Florence, the cradle of the rebirth, and I will soon be
reborn

ELI & HANNA: I fell

ELI: Like a man from a bridge
Which in the dark looks like a comet

ELI & HANNA: I was born with a little light at the bottom of my heart

HANNA: I look at you without even understanding how it is possible

ELI & HANNA: The light of the night
A myriad of explosions that dilate your pupils

ELI: Is this hell?
Burn to death but everything in your arms is better
I am seventeen years old and I have a pack of dreams in my pocket
where others keep cigarettes
I know that inside you there are also

HANNA: two hundred thousand   ELI: duecentomila sogni
dreams

HANNA: I dedicate this smile to the person I love
There is no religion that can tell me who to love

ELI: There is no man in the world who can make me feel once again

ELI & HANNA: a stupid atom of loneliness
So, as always, I put the weight of

HANNA: two hundred thousand   ELI: duecentomila

ELI & HANNA: losses on my shoulders and set off for what are my

HANNA: Dreams.   ELI: Sogni.

Pause.

> *HANNA is overwhelmed.*

ELI: . . . It's better in Italian.

> *A moment.*

> *HANNA and ELI begin to move towards one another, temporarily free
> from the realities of time and space, when suddenly their phones go
> off, tearing them back to the real world. The stars blink out.*

> *They both stop. Look at their phones.*

HANNA: Congratulations. Your campaign is . . . fully funded.

ELI: TheKatV shared a photo of you.

> *Lights out.*

Scene Seven

One week later.

ELI enters.

He has a black eye. His lip is bruised.

He goes to the front of the stage and lights all the white candles. He begins painting his face, but this time, he is doing female drag. He covers the bruising with lipstick and powder. He is seriously shaken.

The sound of a door opening and closing.

ELI: Hello?

The candles flicker.

. . . Hello?

A spider drops from the ceiling and onto ELI's lap. He jumps to his feet.

AGH.

A few moments. The spider doesn't move.

For a moment, ELI considers killing them.

Maybe they're already dead.

Finally, he gets a cup and coerces the spider into it.

He slips a piece of paper under the cup and is about to go outside to release them when MATTEO enters.

Silence.

MATTEO: Does dad know?

ELI: No. He doesn't have Instagram. He didn't see the GoFundMe, he . . . he doesn't know yet.

> *Beat.* ELI *tries to hold steady—to keep the spider under the cup without crushing them.*

MATTEO: That cover-up is the wrong shade. Too dark. You look like you're wearing one of those masks.

ELI: What do you know about makeup?

MATTEO: I know more than you. What's with the cup?

> *Beat.*

ELI: Matteo. I know you're upset. Maybe you have questions? Whatever you want to ask me, I'll / try to explain—

MATTEO: Why didn't you tell me?

> *Beat.*

ELI: Things are complicated right now. There's too much happening at once. Inside. Outside. All around us, there's so much happening—

MATTEO: Why hasn't Dad come home? No bullshit.

ELI: I told you already, his work trip was extended . . .

MATTEO: Do you ever say anything real?

ELI: Matteo . . .

MATTEO: And what if he finds out about you.

Pause.

ELI: Don't tell him. Matteo. Please. Promise me you won't tell him. Not yet. Promise. It has to come from me. Do you understand? I can't . . . I need to have some control.

Beat.

You're right, I should have told you sooner, I'm sorry, but I didn't . . . I didn't have the words, the language, I . . . I still don't. I'm not ready. Matteo, I'm not ready. Do you understand?

Beat.

Please? Please, promise me? Promise you won't tell him.

Pause.

Dad has a girlfriend. In Rome. I think it's serious.

MATTEO exits.

Matteo wait, I'm sorry I—

Beat.

ELI crumples, dropping the cup and the spider. The spider crawls away.

He mumbles the following prayer under his breath, rapid-fire, over and over.

O Gesù, perdona le nostre colpe, preservaci dal fuoco dell'inferno, porta in cielo tutte le anime, specialmente le più bisognose della tua misericordia. O Gesù, perdona le nostre colpe, preservaci dal fuoco dell'inferno, porta in cielo tutte le anime, specialmente le più bisognose della tua misericordia. O Gesù . . .

One by one, the candles along the edge of the stage blink out.

ELI repeats the prayer in darkness.

He stops.

Silence.

Act Two

Winter

Scene Eight

Late December. We are at MATTEO *and* ELI's *apartment in Florence.*

KAT stands in the lobby, staring at the buzzers. She's overdressed.

MATTEO runs on, headed for the mailbox. He stops short when he sees KAT.

Pause. They recognize each other.

MATTEO: Posso aiutarla?

KAT: . . . Matteo?

MATTEO shrugs.

(in halting Italian) Sto cercando Eli. Eliana.

MATTEO shrugs.

Io sono Kat. Katerina.

Beat.

Noi siamo . . . *cugini.* Us. Noi. Cousins.

MATTEO hesitates, shrugs.

Mi piacerebbe . . . vedere Eli.

Beat.

Okay you speak English, right?

MATTEO shrugs.

I wrote down the address wrong. I put a two instead of a five, because of fucking course, so I went to the house across the street but no one was home except this angry little dog so I just like, sat down on the sidewalk, and everybody just walked past me, like somehow not tripping on the cobblestones in their three-inch stilettos but also not offering me any help even though I am so obviously not from here?

Beat.

Eventually this old guy with the most aggressive nose hair I've ever seen took pity on me and told me you live in this building, but only after watching me from his front porch for like half an hour which was . . . creepy. And then I get in here and realize: I don't know the unit number. It was hard enough digging up the address from my dad's old address book and like, I half figured your dad would have moved by now so ANYWAYS I guess what I'm saying is: I'm happy to see you. Like. Relieved, actually.

Pause.

MATTEO: No.

Beat.

KAT: What?

MATTEO: No. You can't see Eliana.

Beat.

KAT: Okay, little man. I know Italy still has some pretty backwards gender norms going on and you probably think you're some kinda de facto family patriarch now that your dad has fucked off to Rome but I have been awake for OVER thirty hours on a pilgrimage to get here that included being harassed by *multiple* border cops and security guards and I am simply not going to take shit from you, so you had better tell me where Eli is before I kick your scrawny fucking ass.

MATTEO turns to leave.

Hey! Where are you going?

MATTEO: Inside.

KAT: You know we're family, too.

Beat.

MATTEO: I hate my family.

MATTEO exits.

KAT: Hey! HEY.

Beat.

Fucking shithead.

KAT waits a few minutes. When it becomes clear that MATTEO *is not coming back, she goes to the buzzer. She doesn't know which buzzer to hit, so she starts hitting them at random, with both fists.*

AEEEEE! Let! Me! Up! I! Have! Been! Awake! THIRTY! TWO! HOURS! LET! ME—

ELI enters, MATTEO *on his heels.* ELI *stops when he sees KAT. She sees him. She lets her fists drop.*

MATTEO: *(to ELI)* Te l'ho detto che non era nessuno!

ELI: Beh, hai mentito, vero?

MATTEO: Sto cercando di proteggerti!

ELI: *Tu* sei il bambino, non io!

MATTEO: Non sono un bambino!

ELI: Ti comporti decisamente come / se lo fossi!

KAT: ENGLISH. PLEASE.

Beat. MATTEO *and* ELI *look at her.*

Could we all please . . . English?

ELI: I thought you were learning Italian.

KAT: Yeah. I'm *learning.*

Beat.

ELI: What do you want.

KAT: This. To speak to you. To know you're still, like . . .

ELI: See? Now what? You go back to Canada?

KAT: After you made that post on Instagram. We thought . . . I had to know that you were okay.

Beat.

I'm sorry. I'm so sorry. I didn't mean for things to happen like they did. I was trying to help.

MATTEO: How did you even arrive here?

Beat.

KAT: I . . . used the money. I thought, since you . . . since you weren't going to use it. That I would finally come . . . meet you in person.

MATTEO: *(to ELI)* Avresti dovuto dirmelo tu per prima. Non questa stupida puttana.

ELI: *(to MATTEO)* Dai, dai!

MATTEO exits.

Beat.

KAT: He doesn't like me.

ELI: He doesn't know you.

KAT: *You* don't like me.

ELI: I am not sure I know you.

Beat.

KAT: I was so worried about you. We were both so worried about you, Hanna and I.

Beat.

Can I hug you? Do you even like hugs? It's weird—I feel like I've already hugged you, in a way, even though that's like obviously impossible, I feel like it isn't, like it's entirely possible, like it's happened before. In a past life.

KAT moves to hug ELI. He pulls away from her.

ELI: I do not believe in reincarnation.

Beat. He gestures to her backpack.

Only this?

KAT: I didn't want to pay for extra luggage. It was like, fifty bucks a bag. Plus, we used to camp a lot. My dads and me.

Beat.

Look, I . . . I fucked up. Really badly. I know that. And you don't need to forgive me, like, not now or like, not ever! You don't, like. Owe me that. But . . . I owed you this. An apology. Face-to-face.

When I made the post, I didn't realize . . . I thought, since you told *me* and since like, your Instagram handle says *Eli* and like you've posted pictures of the rainbow flag and all that stuff about gay rights in Italy, that . . . I'm sorry. I'm really really really sorry. I don't think I'll ever not feel like shit about this.

Beat.

I was thinking on the plane ride over about how our dads were only a little older than us when they stopped talking. Kinda weird, hey? Do you think it means something?

Beat.

ELI: Stronzo.

KAT: What?

ELI: It means you are bad. A bad poo.

Beat.

KAT: Eli, what can I say, what can I do to / make things—

ELI: I walk.

KAT: Oh. Okay . . .

> *He approaches KAT. She softens, relieved—but he's only handing her his apartment key. He exits.*
>
> *KAT goes up to the apartment. She stands for a few moments, taking it in. Maybe she picks up a few things, puts them back down. She starts to unpack.*
>
> *MATTEO enters. He watches without her noticing. She turns around and sees him.*

Jesus! You scared me. How long have you been standing there?

Silence.

Eli let me up. He gave me his key. See?"

MATTEO: Are you adopted?

    Beat.

KAT: . . . I'm your biological cousin, if that's what you're asking.

    Silence. He stares at her until she snaps.

All right, all right, fine! Jesus. Not that it is *any* of your business, but my mother was a surrogate. Okay? Is that what you wanted to know?

MATTEO: You are not Italian.

KAT: Yes, I am. I literally just told you: my dad, your uncle, paid a woman who needed the money to feed the kids she already had, and then some doctor shot my dad's sperm into her vagina with a turkey baster or something and nine months later—tada!—me.

MATTEO: If you are Italian, then I am Canadian?

KAT: What? No. That's doesn't make any—

MATTEO: Eliana told me you were like this.

KAT: . . . Like what?

    The buzzer goes off, startling KAT.

    MATTEO exits.

    She buzzes ELI up.

    He enters.

How was your walk?

ELI: No.

KAT: Oh . . . kay.

ELI: I will be ready. But not now.

> *Beat.*

I want to forgive you. But not . . . yet.

> *Beat.*

KAT: I got you a few things. You don't have to . . . we don't have to talk, but . . . I want to give them to you. Then I'll go out and give you some space. Promise.

> *KAT roots through her bags. She takes out two binders: a school bind-er, and a chest binder.*

BINDERS!

> *Beat.*

Get it? Y'know, like? Word play? This is a binder . . . but this is *also* a binder?

> *Beat.*

(referring to the chest binder) I don't know if you already have one or not by now, but I remembered when you said you wanted to try binding, so . . . I bought it from this really cool site that specializes in trans healthcare and . . . okay. Sorry. Here. If this is even, like. Still a thing you want.

ELI takes the chest binder. He holds it throughout the following.

(referring to the school binder) And then . . . I did some research. About how to medically transition in Italy. If that's something you still want. I know that, like. Stuff changes. And not all trans people want to be on hormones or whatever but I remembered you talking about it and how you said you'd never talked about it with anybody else before and so I thought maybe . . .

Beat.

Why don't you just . . . take this. And then you can look at it in your own time. If you want to.

ELI doesn't take it. He is still holding the chest binder.

. . . Okay. I'll just. Leave it.

KAT puts the binder down.

She exits.

Once she is gone, ELI risks a glance at it.

He picks it up.

Flips it open to the first page.

Scene Nine

Shift.

All four characters are on stage.

ELI: It's November. It's raining. It's been nine days. Two hundred hours. Two hundred hours since the world found out about . . . since my father . . .

KAT: I leave Eli's apartment and I just . . . go. I know I'm going to get totally lost, but I tell myself: Florence isn't that big, geographically speaking. Toronto's way bigger.

ELI: I'm at confession. I half expect to burn up as soon as I set foot over the threshold of the church but . . . I don't.

KAT: And I'm walking, power walking or speed walking or whatever, and I guess I'm not totally watching where I'm going because I trip.

ELI: I thought it would feel wrong, to be here, surrounded by the stained-glass saints and the pews and the smell of—wood? Some kind of wood I can't name, something brought here from far away, but . . . it doesn't.

KAT: I trip and I fall right onto the steps of a church. Which, okay, not that big of a coincidence, right? Cuz like. Italy. Churches are like Starbucks here. But the doors are open, these big scary-looking doors, the kind with brass handles, and I can hear music. Someone is playing piano.

ELI: It's been six months since my last confession. I can't even remember what I confessed to. When you're lying about something so enormous, everything else feels inconsequential. Maybe I made something up.

KAT: It smells . . . old, inside. But not in a bad way. Old, like . . . the way my grandpa's sweaters used to smell when he hugged me to his stomach. Or like, a cave. And I think . . . fuck it. This is my history, right? My culture? Like it or not.

ELI: I've known this priest since I was a child. When my mother died, he came to our home. I was ten. Matteo was only five, maybe six. I'd made him take a pact with me, not to speak to anyone, not even our father. I was his big sibling. He did what I said.

KAT: It's dim and dusty inside and I have to squint till my eyes adjust, but then . . . wow. Holy crap. This place is fucked up. Like, fucked up beautiful. But also like, *fucked up* fucked up. Hyperrealistic statues of saints all full of arrows and bleeding out of their eyes and being stoned to death and shit. It's . . . violent.

ELI: No one could get us to speak . . . until the priest. He didn't save us with prayer, like my father wanted him to. Instead, he brought us toys. *His* toys, from when he was a child. Little plastic army men, a tank on wheels, the kind you wind up and send shooting forwards.

KAT: And then I see him. The man playing piano. Except it's not a piano, it's an . . . organ. He's wearing a long white robe the same colour as his hair. We're . . . alone. In this huge dark space. Alone. There are so many people outside, but not in here. I am suddenly very aware of how far I've wandered, how far away the door is. And then he turns and sees me and—

ELI: Eventually—after weeks and weeks of visiting us at our house— the priest convinced Matteo and I to come back to church. We hadn't been since our mother's funeral. I was scared. I didn't want to go back. But he held my hand. My father never held my hand, but the priest did. He held my hand all the way to the confessional.

KAT: He looks exactly like my nonno. I never met him, my non- no—only saw my dad's old photos—but it's . . . spooky. Those long dark eyelashes and that white white hair. And this old guy who looks exactly like my dead nonno smiles and I swear to fucking god his eyes *twinkle* and he says: "Are you ready to confess?"

Beat.

How does it start, again?

Beat.

ALL: Bless me Father, for I have sinned.

ELI, MATTEO, & KAT: I have watched pornography.

ELI: I have driven drunk.
I have lied to my younger brother.

ALL: I have kissed a boy.

ELI: I have hated kissing a boy.

ELI & KAT: I have lied to my father.

ALL: I have lied to my friends.

ELI: I have sought absolution from strangers on the Internet.
I have killed a spider when I could have spared its life because people were watching.

ALL: I have touched myself.

ELI & KAT: I have touched myself . . . often.

ELI: I have fantasized about having a cock while I touched myself.

I have called a girl I've never spoken to before a slut because people were listening.

I have fantasized about having sex with the girl I called a slut because maybe she would understand.

Because maybe we are the same.

ELI & HANNA: I have thought about suicide.

KAT: I have betrayed someone I love in the worst possible way.

> *Beat. MATTEO, KAT, and HANNA exit.*

ELI: And I can't see the priest's face, I can't see his face because I'm kneeling beside an opaque screen but I can hear the smile in his voice and I can picture the wrinkles around his eyes and I can feel God there with us.

"The Church needs more people like you," he says. "With spirits like . . . you."

> *Shift.*

Scene Ten

> *One day after Scene Eight.*

> *MATTEO, ELI, and KAT arrive back at the apartment. They are all a little tipsy. KAT has a brown paper bag with liquor in it.*

KAT: How do you DO it? How is it humanly possible?

ELI: Practice.

MATTEO: I could eat forever and never stop.

KAT: I'm dead.

MATTEO: *(to KAT)* You are *weak.*

KAT: Nope. Definitely dead.

ELI: I'm going to shower. It is too hot! Too hot!

MATTEO: Good. You stink:

> *ELI flips him off and exits.*

> *KAT takes the bottle out of the brown paper bag.*

KAT: I can't believe that was so *easy!* Do they really never card here?

> *MATTEO shrugs.*

> *KAT pours them each a glass.*

Here. *(she holds it away from him)* But only if you hang out with me.

> *MATTEO hesitates but takes the glass.*

MATTEO: Eliana said you made a deal with the Devil.

KAT: What? No. I mean, I guess I did, like, give him my credit card.

MATTEO: *Satan?*

KAT: No, no, not Satan—the guy who runs the Satanic Temple. They're not, like, an actual faith group. They're activists. They don't worship the Devil, if that's what you're worried about.

MATTEO: You gave these people money for . . . what?

KAT: Ummm, it was for . . . a T-shirt with a pentagram on it? But the funds went to a pro-choice legal fund. Or something. The Satanic Temple is always staging these protests about reproductive rights. Like, a couple of years ago, they dressed up in leather and giant baby heads to protest a protest of Planned Parenthood. Like. To protest against people who want to make abortions illegal in America.

MATTEO: They protest for . . . abortions?

KAT: Yeah, basically. So women—sorry—so people with uteruses can actually, like, have access.

Beat.

Does that bother you?

Beat.

MATTEO: A girl in my grade got pregnant last year.

Beat.

She didn't want the baby. Her parents made her move to Ugnano with her grandparents.

KAT: Shit. Sorry.

MATTEO: We weren't friends.

Pause.

Eliana says you like girls.

KAT: I do.

MATTEO: . . . *And* boys.

KAT: I do. And—before you ask. No. It's not a "phase."

MATTEO: Una *bisessuale*.

KAT: Bisexual. Yep. Or pansexual, whatever.

> *Beat.*

MATTEO: There's a boy in my school. Niccolo.

KAT: Oh! Is he your boy—

MATTEO: No! No, no, no.

KAT: Okay.

> *Beat.*

MATTEO: We kissed. At a party. It was a game, spin the bottle, but we . . . he kissed me.

KAT: And did you . . . like it?

> *Beat.*

MATTEO: Is it the same?

KAT: Is what the / same?

MATTEO: Is it the same for you with girls as boys. Kissing. Does it feel . . . different?

> *Beat.*

If I make it so you cannot / see—

KAT: kinky

MATTEO: —and someone kisses you, could you say, "this is a boy" or "this is a girl."

KAT: Umm. I think . . . I think it's more about the person? It's more like. Oh yeah, this is Simon kissing me, because he likes to shove his tongue right in there, no preamble. Or . . . yeah, yeah that's Dale, because Dale does a duck face when they kiss, like they're posing for a selfie. Or, this must be Max, because she likes to bite, only a little, suck on my lower lip *just* hard enough that it hurts but not hard enough to make me bleed.

> *Beat.*

Soooooo. Yeah. Kissing is more about the person than their gender. For me.

> *Pause.*

MATTEO: When we kissed, Niccolo and I, on Halloween . . . one of the other boys, Alessandro. He did a . . . *(he mimes videotaping)*

KAT: He filmed it? That's fucked up, man.

MATTEO: And he put it on Instagram. Eliana told me . . . Eliana says he is gay. Alessandro.

KAT: Honestly, like nine times out of ten homophobes *are* gay.

MATTEO: Homo—?

KAT: Homophobes. Kids who bully gay kids. Or, like. Adults who bully gay adults.

MATTEO: Ninety percent . . . gay? How do you know this?

KAT: I mean, like. I don't know if it's actually *ninety* percent. Scientifically speaking. But there was a study done and yeah, homophobes are definitely like, at least more *likely* to be gay.

> *Beat.*

MATTEO: After Niccolo and I kissed . . . we start to escape each other. In the hallways. After school. An understanding, we have a . . . neither of us speaks, but. We know. We cannot. Not anymore.

KAT: You can't . . . ?

> *Beat.*

MATTEO: Every week, after school, he comes over. Not on Mondays or Wednesdays or Fridays because on Mondays he does football and on Wednesdays he does piano and on Fridays he goes to stay in Pisa but every Tuesday and Thursday.

> *Beat.*

Not anymore. We cannot. We pretend not to see each other in the hallway, and in gym we are on opposite teams. He plays in attacco. Me, I am in difesa. And he trips me without even looking. Scores. His feet . . . confusa. His face . . . confusa. I am on the ground and my shoulder, it hurts. It hurts now, even.

> *Beat.*

We cannot. We cannot . . . I cannot . . .

KAT: Matteo. What? What can't you?

MATTEO: In my bedroom . . . a joke. Niccolo says, What if? We laugh. Me, I pretend to be only curious, I say, "Oh, I've never seen this one before," I say, "*che paio di finocchi.*" He says, "What if?" We try. Me, I still pretend, I say, "It feels like nothing, I feel nothing." He says, "What if?" And then he is . . . his hands . . . And he asks again: "Still nothing? You feel nothing?"

> *Beat.*

The entire time, in my bedroom: no kissing. Never. We never kiss, not until we spin the bottle, because . . . because if we never kiss, we can do what we want. And I feel nothing.

> *Pause.*

> *KAT goes to MATTEO. He's crying softly.*

KAT: I'm going to hug you now. Okay?

> *She hugs him. He resists at first, but then lets her.*

> *Several moments.*

> *ELI enters, wrapped in a towel.*

ELI: What's going on?

(to KAT) Did you give him *more*? He was already drunk!

KAT: He's fifteen!

ELI: *Fourteen!*

The buzzer rings loudly.

MATTEO: Who . . . ?

The buzzer rings again. MATTEO jumps to his feet.

Is it—

ELI: No, no. It is not . . . *our* father . . .

Beat. It sinks in.

KAT: Ohmygod, you did NOT tell my dads I was here—

ELI: It was Hanna! Hanna told them! It was / not me—

KAT: That fucking *bitch*—

ELI: You told them you were at her home without telling her of your plan to get on the plane, to come here—what did you believe would / happen—

KAT: I should've *known* you two were still sexting—

MATTEO: What?

ELI: We never did this "sexting"!

KAT: I can't believe this.

The buzzer rings again.

(to ELI) Don't you dare.

ELI goes to the buzzer, pushes it.

You are so lucky I have no moral high ground right now.

A few moments.

A knock at the door.

ELI *answers it.*

It is HANNA.

Pause.

Ummm. Hello?

HANNA: You are in such deep shit.

KAT: With who, exactly? You?

HANNA: Your dads! They're checking in at a hotel down the street right now. They sent me to get you.

KAT: BOTH of them?

HANNA: Yes, *both of them*! The only reason they didn't come with me is because they thought your uncle might be here. And I told them you'd put up less of a fight if it was just me, which they know is true. Frank wanted to come anyways, but I talked him down, convinced him to stay behind with Francesco.

MATTEO: . . . Your dads' names are . . . Frank and Francesco?

KAT: Don't.

MATTEO: Do they *know*—

KAT: This is so not the time.

> *HANNA and ELI cannot stop staring at one another, even while they are speaking to MATTEO and KAT.*

ELI: *(to HANNA)* Why . . . how are you here?

HANNA: I convinced my mom to let me come with. She almost got on the plane with us, she was so freaked out.

(to KAT) She's been sending me a text once every, like, ten minutes asking if you're all right.

> *ELI and HANNA start to instinctively move towards each other.*

ELI: You're here.

HANNA: Can I—?

KAT: Yeah, nice to see you, too.

MATTEO: What are you doing?

> *ELI and HANNA freeze.*

MATTEO: *(to HANNA)* Che cazzo stai facendo con mia sorella?

ELI: Matteo, back off.

> *HANNA's cellphone goes off. She answers it.*

HANNA: Hello? Yes, I'm sorry—I know. I'm here with her now.

MATTEO: *(to ELI)* Why? La conosci?

HANNA: Yeah, she's totally fine.

MATTEO: *(to ELI)* Bene. More secrets, hey?

HANNA: *(to KAT)* Francesco wants to talk to you.

KAT: Hell no.

HANNA: You have to stop making me your middleman!

KAT: Oh, I'm sorry—did I involve you? Did I make you my middleman, or did you decide that for yourself? Kind of funny, isn't it, given that not too long ago YOU were lecturing ME about not involving yourself where you're CLEARLY not wanted—

> *They have a silent exchange, along the lines of, "Take the phone!" "No!" "Take it!" "NO!" until HANNA forces it into KAT's hands.*

KAT: . . . Dad?

> *KAT holds the phone away from her ear.*

HANNA: You're Matteo, right? I've heard a lot about you—

MATTEO: Who are you?

> *Beat.*

ELI: *(to HANNA)* You don't have to explain yourself / to him—

KAT: *(into the phone)* Look, I didn't ASK you to come here! I didn't ASK you to spend all that money!

HANNA: *(to ELI)* It's okay.

KAT: I didn't ask you to have me in the first place! Jesus, would you stop LORDING it over me like I CHOSE to be your kid—

HANNA: I'm Hanna.

KAT: Well maybe if you'd actually *brought* me here, like, YEARS ago, maybe if you'd actually introduced me to my family instead of keeping me hidden from them like some kind of—

MATTEO spits on HANNA.

MATTEO: Vai a cacare.

Silence.

KAT shoves the cellphone into ELI's hands and attacks MATTEO. They wrestle. HANNA and ELI try to pry them apart with little success.

KAT: WHAT DID YOU SAY TO HER, YOU LITTLE / PIECE OF—

HANNA: Hey hey hey HEY!

ELI: *(into the phone)* Uhhh, pronto, Kat will call you back?!

All four characters' dialogue overlaps here. Actors may feel free to ad lib. HANNA's cellphone rings throughout the following.

ELI: Stop it, stop it you two, you are drunk—	HANNA: This is ridiculous, what are you even—
KAT: STRONZO, STRONZO, STRONZO—	MATTEO: Puttana, qual è il tuo problemo—
ELI: You idiot, è la mia ragazza—	HANNA: Peace not violence! Peace not violence!!

KAT: STRONZO, STRONZO, STRONO—   MATTEO: Vaffanculo!

HANNA: *(answering the phone)*   ELI: Sei un uomo morto, scendi da
Hi, I'm sorry, yes we're fine, can I   lei! Get off her!
call you—

KAT: I DON'T CARE how homophobic   MATTEO: Pensi di conoscere me-
your culture is, you do NOT get to   glio Eli di me?
treat—

    ELI *manages to pry* MATTEO *and* KAT *apart.*

HANNA: Yes, Kat is just PACKING HER BAGS NOW. Uh-huh. Okay. Sorry,
yes, we're totally fine it's just that we're—so—*excited* to see each other!
Okay! Yes! Okay! See you soon.

    HANNA *hangs up.*

    Beat.

Kat, he's a CHILD, you can't / attack a—

MATTEO: I AM NOT A / CHILD—

KAT: Ummm, he *spat* on you?! I'm trying to DEFEND you, / don't you—

HANNA: Yeah, well maybe if you spent less time trying to defend other
people and more time reflecting on your own *freaking actions* we
wouldn't BE / in this huge—

ELI: SHUT UP SHUT UP SHUT UP SHUT UP SHUT UP.
COULD YOU ALL SHUT THE FUCK UP.
JUST
SHUT
UP.

Beat.

Can we just. Be quiet. For a while?

Silence.

(to KAT) I don't want to be like our fathers.

KAT: We're not!

ELI: Look at us! Look at you two!

Beat.

There's a belief that . . . it is impossible to translate poetry. Because the art form, the . . . the *meaning* of the language does not cross over. To translate a poem is to create a new piece of art.

Beat.

KAT: Did that make sense to anybody else?

ELI: I am tired. I cannot keep . . . translating myself. I need someone to tell me they see me and *mean* it—

HANNA: Can I kiss you?

ELI nods. HANNA kisses him, hard.

MATTEO and KAT look away.

HANNA's cellphone goes off again.

MATTEO answers it.

MATTEO: Pronto?

KAT grabs it from him.

KAT: Hi. Yes. Yeah. I'm actually coming.

Beat.

I'm sorry. I know. I know, I'm the worst, okay? Yes, I'm a horrible person, I get it. I already know, I don't need you to tell me aga— What? You can't threaten me with—that is NOT fair—FINE FINE FINE OKAY BYE.

Beat.

He's threatening to use my college fund on a trip to Prague. So.

KAT waits for a response from HANNA, ELI, anyone, but no one acknowledges her. She groans and exits.

ELI: I thought it would be different. You, here. But . . .

HANNA: I know. It's not.

ELI and HANNA hold each other.

KAT returns with her bag, hastily thrown together. She stops at MATTEO.

KAT: *(to MATTEO)* I'm sorry I hit you, even if you were being a total dick. I'm a pacifist. It's against my values.

Beat.

Tell him, okay? Sooner, rather than later.

(to ELI) Thanks for hiding me. Even if you did also break my cover. Oh, and I have probably forgotten at *least* two things here, so if you could—

HANNA: Kat.

KAT: —mail those to me that'd be great kthanksbye!

> *KAT starts to exit, but ELI stops her and hugs her. A moment.*
>
> *KAT and HANNA exit.*
>
> *MATTEO and ELI look at one another.*
>
> *ELI exits.*
>
> *MATTEO climbs onto the couch. He falls asleep.*
>
> *He keeps sleeping.*

Spring

Scene Eleven

> *HANNA and ELI are both presenting class projects.*
>
> *The lighting of the stage slowly transforms from cool to warm.*

ELI: Pope Francis's views on LGBT people have been celebrated by some gay, lesbian, and trans people. But the Pope has said a number of things that lead me to feel skeptical of his support for the queer community.

HANNA: Lake Urmia, in Iran, is the example pointed to most often to demonstrate the ways in which climate change is altering the mosaics of Earth's waters.

ELI: In 2015, the Pope said: "Let's think of the nuclear arms, of the possibility to annihilate in a few instants a very high number of human beings."

HANNA: In just four months, the waters of Lake Urmia transformed from deep green to blood red.

ELI: "Let's think also of genetic manipulation, of the manipulation of life, or of gender theory, that does not recognize the *order* of creation."

HANNA: The water's high salt concentration has made it the perfect breeding ground for *Dunaliella* algae, a form of algae that uses a red pigment to absorb the sun's rays. Lake Urmia's surface area has shrunk by seventy percent in the last fourteen years alone.

ELI: Earlier that same year, he said: "The family is threatened by growing efforts on the part of some to redefine the very institution of marriage—by the culture of the ephemeral, by a lack of openness to *life*."

HANNA & ELI: In conclusion,

HANNA: To quote Hossein Akhani, "If land use and water consumption remain as they are now, then the lake will disappear pretty soon."

ELI: If the Catholic Church believes that queer families, trans lives, that all of this is a threat to life—how do we, queer Catholics, interpret this? Does the Pope want us to disappear? How do we live?

HANNA and KAT graduate high school in Toronto.

ELI graduates high school in Florence.

MATTEO sleeps.

KAT packs for university.

HANNA packs to travel.

ELI administers his first shot of testosterone to his upper thigh.

MATTEO sleeps.

ELI packs his bags.

KAT exits.

HANNA exits.

MATTEO continues to sleep.

Summer

Scene Twelve

ELI wakes MATTEO.

ELI: Hey.

MATTEO: Mfffff.

ELI: It's two o'clock.

MATTEO: Fuck off.

ELI: Matteo. I'm leaving.

MATTEO rolls away from him.

This is how you want to say goodbye?

Beat.

I offered to buy you a ticket. It's not too late. The Airbnb has a pull-out couch.

MATTEO: As much as I would love to spend a romantic month with you and your girlfriend—no.

ELI: Matteo, come on. You've always wanted to visit Venice, since you were this big. Pulling mom's hair? Begging her to take you? You were convinced the lions must come alive when no one was watching. That statues could spread their wings and soar over the city. That it must be magic, a city on water. Remember?

Beat.

MATTEO: You're only going because she's making you. You could be going to the coast, or the mountains, but instead you're going to be suffocated by Americans in khakis and the military with their guns and bird shit.

Beat.

ELI: Have you tried talking to—

MATTEO: Dad would have come back if it weren't for you.

ELI: I talked to dad yesterday. Rent is all paid, until the new year. Utilities, too. He gave me his address in Rome.

Beat.

And . . . Kat is coming to stay with you while I'm gone.

MATTEO: *(finally sitting up)* What?!

ELI: I knew you wouldn't come with me, so I asked if she wanted to come stay for the summer, rent free. While Hanna and I are away. To make sure you don't do anything stupid. She'll be here tonight.

MATTEO: I don't need a babysitter!

ELI: You're fifteen . . .

> *Beat.*

Dad says he'll visit soon . . .

MATTEO: You mean as soon as his girlfriend will let him. Which is never.

> *Beat.*

Do you think she's pregnant?

> *Beat.*

I hope it's a stillborn.

ELI: *Matteo.*

> *Pause.*

I left you a couple of beers. Don't drink too much at once. Remember last year? Halloween?

MATTEO: No.

ELI: You were dressed like a gondolier? Cute little scarf? Your peach fuzz was just starting to come in? You puked on mom's grave, then went comatose the rest of the day?

Beat.

Niccolo?

MATTEO: I don't remember.

ELI: Okay. Sure. Fine. You know, this actually explains a lot! You have amnesia! That's why you don't respect it when I tell you over and over and over which pronouns I use, what my name is. That's why you don't respect it when I try to take care of you. Cook you food, do your laundry. You've forgotten everything except yourself.

Pause.

I'm leaving now.

Pause.

Be good, Matteo. I love you.

ELI hesitates a moment longer.

MATTEO does not look at him.

ELI exits.

Shift.

Later the same day.

KAT enters with a suitcase.

MATTEO is moaning on the ground.

MATTEO: I am going to hell.

KAT: Nice to see you, too. Can this crisis of morality wait two seconds for me to pee? Because I've been holding it since the luggage drop-off.

MATTEO nods.

KAT exits.

KAT returns and begins unloading candles, crystals, etc., from her bag.

MATTEO: What are you doing?

KAT: If you're going to have a mental breakdown, we'll need to do a cleanse.

MATTEO: I am not breaking.

KAT: Hey, no judgment. I have mental breakdowns all the time.

Beat.

Okay, well like, not *all* the time. But I've been there. Especially last year.

MATTEO: Before or after you showed up at our apartment?

KAT: Before.

Beat.

And after. Anyway, it's nothing to be ashamed of. C'mon.

KAT lays a blanket on the ground. MATTEO sits with her.

Talk.

MATTEO: I think . . . I am a . . . faggot.

KAT: Okay?

MATTEO makes a "so I'm going to hell!!?" gesture.

You know literally nobody cares, right? And I mean that in the most loving way possible, but—nobody cares.

MATTEO: I care!

KAT picks up one of the crystals.

KAT: Stay still.

She starts rubbing the crystal against his temples.

MATTEO: What the—?!

KAT: Still.

MATTEO: Does this have to do with Satan?

KAT: No, Satan has not blessed these crystals, okay? Besides, you're already gay. What more could he do to you?

MATTEO jerks away.

Joking, joking!

Beat.

Listen, you don't have to know what you are right now. Labels are only useful when they're useful. It's okay to take some time to figure things out.

Beat.

This is quartz. It's good for banishing negative energy and clearing your mind.

MATTEO: You really believe this?

KAT: You really believe you're going to hell for liking boys?

Beat.

Breathe.

MATTEO closes his eyes and breathes. Several moments of this.

Do you like baths?

MATTEO: I haven't had a bath since I was a baby.

KAT: I always wished I had a sibling when I was little. So I'd have someone to take baths with. Someone to splash.

MATTEO: Our mom used to make Eli and I have baths together.

KAT: You said Eli.

Beat.

I'm going to draw you a detox bath. You need to soak for at least thirty minutes. Try to just keep breathing. Here, smell this. Lavender. Nice?

She holds some under his nose to smell. He nods, tentative.

Great. Take these *(she lifts the white candles from the edge of the stage)* and light them once you get in.

KAT exits.

The sound of bathwater running.

MATTEO stares at the white candles. Suddenly, they light themselves.

MATTEO: Argh!

KAT returns.

KAT: You're not supposed to light those until you get INTO the bath, dingus.

MATTEO: But I didn't—

KAT: Did you go through my bag for matches?

MATTEO: No, they just—

KAT: *(spotting the matches sitting on the blanket amidst an array of crystals, scents, etc.)* Oh, I left them out. Sorry, I can't help it. I'm like a tornado. I've been here two seconds and it's like—whoosh!

MATTEO is still staring at the candles.

Go on. The water's running. Don't wanna flood the apartment.

MATTEO picks up the candles, tentative.

MATTEO: Kat?

KAT: Mhm?

MATTEO: I said some things to Eli, before she—he—

KAT: Matteo. You're fifteen. Nobody expects you to be a good person yet. Your brain isn't even fully formed.

> *Beat.*

MATTEO: You are an asshole.

KAT: See? I give you sage advice, what do you do? Insult me! No respect for your elders!

> *MATTEO rolls his eyes, exits.*

(calling after him) Don't worry, one day you'll be eighteen and it'll allllllll make sense!

> *MATTEO takes a bath. He relaxes. Breathing in lavender. Watching the candles flicker.*

> *KAT reads from an English–Italian dictionary.*

> *HANNA and ELI are on a bridge in Venice.*

HANNA: A long time ago you asked me if I believe in God.

ELI: Yes.

HANNA: I never answered you.

ELI: No.

HANNA: I didn't know what to tell you. I didn't want to lie.

ELI: And so . . . you are an atheist?

HANNA: No, I'm not.

ELI: Jewish? Muslim?

HANNA: No, I don't . . .

ELI: Buddhist?

HANNA: How do I explain . . .

    Beat.

I do believe in . . . something. A being. A . . . consciousness.

ELI: Cos'e, "consciousness?"

HANNA: Like a . . . superior mind. A mind much, much more complex than ours.

    Beat.

Imagine . . . picture an ant. An ant, it goes about its daily business—foraging for food, carrying it back to the queen, cleaning itself—that's all it knows. Right? An ant's brain is too small to understand any concept more complex than food or sleep.

ELI: Sounds like Matteo.

    Beat.

Do bugs *sleep?*

HANNA: Some do. Fruit flies, cockroaches—they sleep. Others go into this state called "torpor," which is kind of like a self-induced paralysis, or a—

ELI laughs.

ELI: You really know everything.

HANNA: No! That's the point! Ants, they only know what they *need* to know. Humans—we're the same. Do we really *need* to know whether or not there's a God, or a higher power, or whatever? Like, in order to survive, day-to-day?

ELI: Yes.

HANNA: Okay but not *technically*. Technically, your heart will keep beating and your lungs will keep absorbing oxygen and your brain will keep firing off neurons whether or not you know for certain there's a God.

ELI: I don't understand.

HANNA: An ant could never understand human thought. Right?

ELI: Right.

HANNA: We're ants.

Beat.

ELI: I don't—

HANNA: To something else, some other consciousness, *we* are *ants*. We can't even *conceive* of how complex the universe really is. We just don't have the programming, the, the hard-wiring. We're not *built* to understand.

    Beat.

. . . I feel like we're being watched.

ELI: Ignore them.

HANNA: I don't need you to protect me.

    Beat.

Ugh, I am sweating through my clothes right now.

ELI: Maybe *that* is why they stare.

    HANNA wacks him.

Have you been to church on Mass?

HANNA: My family never went to church.

ELI: What about choir? Have you ever done singing in a choir?

HANNA: Oh, I don't sing.

ELI: You don't sing?

HANNA: No.

ELI: Never?

HANNA: No . . .

ELI: Aha!

Beat.

HANNA: What? Why did you say "aha" like that?

ELI: You cannot understand God if you don't sing!

HANNA: That makes literally no sense.

ELI: È come cercare di capire l'italiano senza un dizionario.

HANNA: What?!

ELI: Exactly!

HANNA: Are you making fun of me?

ELI: No, no! Singing is science. You will like this.

HANNA: Okay . . .

ELI: *(relishing the fact that he knows something she doesn't)* The oldest instrument in the world—a flute—was made from the bones of a vulture. Forty thousand years ago! A bone flute. Who taught humans to make music from bones?

HANNA: Where did you read that?

Beat. ELI is embarrassed.

ELI: I have been reading *National Geographic*. Since you sent me that story—

HANNA: Lake Urmia?

ELI: Yes.

HANNA: I didn't know you'd actually read it.

ELI: It made me sad.

HANNA: You were already sad.

> *Beat.*

At least it will be pretty. The blues will become more blue. The greens, more green. Everything will intensify.

ELI: As it dies.

HANNA: As phytoplankton *evolves.*

> *Beat. They watch the water flow under the bridge.*

ELI: Maybe I should be a gondolier.

HANNA: Hmmm . . . you would look cute in the uniform.

ELI: But only once Venice has sunk.

HANNA: Post-apocalyptic tourism? Why not.

> *Lights begin to shift.*

ELI: I will row tourists under bridges, breaking bridges, broken archways

HANNA: Through oceans of bright blue, warm like bathwater

ELI: I will sing to them, to keep them close to God, even once the world has ended

HANNA: You've got to corner the market, though.

Beat.

They hold each other.

This time, ELI is self-conscious, aware of people watching.

HANNA: Ignore them. Remember?

ELI: But . . . as for

KAT: Tomorrow

KAT & ELI: Domani

ELI: Ci sveglieremo e guarderemo

KAT & ELI: L'alba

KAT: The sunrise

KAT & ELI: Mattina

KAT: Morning

KAT & ELI: Pomeriggio

KAT: Afternoon

KAT & ELI: Notte

KAT: Night

ELI: Un mese intero per stare

KAT & ELI: Insieme

Lights fade on KAT, ELI, and HANNA.

MATTEO is lit only by the candles around the edge of the bath.

A few moments of silence.

MATTEO hums to himself; maybe Ultimo's "Il Ballo Delle Incertezze" (The Dance of Uncertainties), the same song ELI sung to him at the beginning of the play. Maybe another song.

As he hums, he blows out each candle, one by one:

Darkness.

End of play.

Acknowledgements

Land

This play was written and rewritten in three different places, each one the traditional homelands of multiple distinct Indigenous Nations. I gratefully welcome corrections to any mistakes or omissions included here.

> Firstly, in Dish With One Spoon treaty territory, on the ancestral lands/waters of the Anishinaabe Nations, the member Nations of the Haudenosaunee Confederacy, and the Wendat;

> Secondly, on the unceded and ancestral lands/waters of the Squamish, Musqueam, and Tsleil-Waututh Nations;

> And thirdly, on the unceded and ancestral lands/waters of the ləkwəŋən and W̱SÁNEĆ peoples. (I use the term "unceded" here because, although some of the Nations on what is now called Southern Vancouver Island orally negotiated treaties with early colonizers that confirmed their right to maintain jurisdiction over their own territories—including ancestors of the Songhees Nation—they were then asked to sign blank pieces of paper confirming these oral agreements. The text of the Douglas Treaties was only written in afterward.)[1]

As an uninvited settler of mixed European ancestry, I'd like to express gratitude to all of the First Nations, Métis, and Inuit people—past, present, and future—who protect and care for these lands and waters. Grazie mille.

---

1 *Douglas Treaties*, Te'mexw Treaty Association, https://temexw.org/moderntreaties/douglas-treaties/.

Friends & Family

Big hugs to everyone who has supported me throughout this process, including (in no particular order): Paula Wing, Judith Thompson, Preeti Kaur Dhaliwal, Sunny Drake, Avery-Jean Brennan, Bilal Baig, Michael Shamata, Zach Cameron, Anna Pappas (and the whole team at Ergo Pink Fest), my cohort in the M.F.A. program at the University of Guelph (especially everyone who stood together with love and kindness during the chaos of that first year playwriting workshop . . .), and my loves: Willow, garo, Mija, and Oscar.

I'm 110% certain that I'm forgetting folks here. But I love you all.

kai fig taddei is a neurotic trans squiggle whose habits include deleting /reinstalling dating apps, forgetting about that tea they poured an hour ago, and catastrophizing. kai wrote this play early in their second puberty, which probably explains all the teenage angst.

First edition: October 2022

Printed and bound in Canada by Rapido Books, Montreal
Cover art by Salini Perera

 PLAYWRIGHTS
CANADA PRESS

202-269 Richmond St. W.
Toronto, ON
M5V 1X1

416.703.0013
info@playwrightscanada.com
www.playwrightscanada.com
@playcanpress